Poems from an Average Girl

Shankayla Tiffany

The first part of this book was written when I was fairly young! Hopefully as you continue to read you will see my growth!

© **COPYRIGHT 2019 - ALL RIGHTS RESERVED.**

DEDICATION

This book is dedicated to every person who has been in love. To anyone who has had their heart broken, wanted to end it all or has felt lost, this book is for you. You are strong, beautiful and important. Follow your dreams and never stop! No matter how many times people may doubt you, criticize you or attempt to break you! Keep pushing. One day those dreams will become a reality. Don't give up. The world needs you!

Love,

Shankayla Tiffany♡

Table of Contents

1. Poems in My Brain

There are poems in my brain
I can't contain.
Some about love and loss,
some about triumph and gain.
Some about hurt and pain,
some about passion and desire.
Some about re-igniting the fire
of a love that was once burnt out.

They all come from the depths of my heart.
Some have no ending,
just a start.
Some about my life,
some about yours.
Some for when you can't find the right words.

These poems are for the average person.
No need to overthink what they are saying,
just feel them.
Take them in.
Fill you up.
Take you away
to that magical place
In your soul.

I'm no Angelou, Shakespeare, Tavon, Jeanty, or
Hughes
No Dickinson, Frost, Poe, Silverstein, or Giovanni,

Walker, Kaur, Baldwin, Morrison, or Lang.
I'm just a girl with poems in my brain.
Enjoy!

2. What Happens When I Fall in Love?

What happens when I fall in love?
I wake up in a good mood.
I'm happy.
I feel wanted.
I feel warm all over.
I dream about him every night.
I can't concentrate in school.
My focus is love.
I feel special, because I know
there is someone out there who loves me.
What happens when I fall in love?
I write poetry.

3. How Do You Know You Are in Love?

How do you know you are in love?
You can feel it in your soul.
You can't wait to call or anticipate their
call.
When you finally hear their voice or think
about them,
you get butterflies.
You draw hearts on almost everything.
Your heart skips a beat when your eyes or
mind sees them.
How do you know you are in love?
You just know.

4. What Does Love Mean to Me?

What does love mean to me?
Caring for someone.
Waking up in a good mood, because I know I
will talk to him.
Being together forever.
Telling each other how we feel.
It means talking and feeling a connection.
To me?
LOVE means EVERYTHING!

5. Can't Wait

He tickled my stomach
I thought I would faint.
I wanted to have someone paint
his beautiful face
on a canvas.
I would stare at it all day long.
I'd stare at it until his face melted off the
wall
And was laying next to me.

6. My Friend

I can't wait to see this boy.
I think about him all day.
When I sleep and dream my sweet dreams,
I see his beautiful face!
I can't place
my finger on why I like him so much.
Maybe,
it's his sexy eyes,
the way he makes them watch my thighs!
Maybe,
it's his lips,
or the way he licks them when he watches my
hips.
I can't wait to see this boy again!
He's just a friend
But I seriously wish he was my man!

7. I'm Ready

I'm ready to hug you
and never let go.
I'm ready to kiss you
and never break loose.
I'm ready to lay down with you
and never get up.
I'm ready to give myself to you
and never share me with another.
I'm ready to give you my all.
I'm ready to be yours forever.

8. He's My EVERYTHING!

He's my heart and my soul.
He's my ball in the goal.
He's my knight in shining armor.
My water to put out any fire.
He's my big blue sky.
The twinkle of my eye.
He's the fruit of my loom.
My bomb, that goes BOOM!
He's my music box.
My foxy red socks.
He's my angel in the sky.
My favorite slice of pie.
He's my paper and pen.
My egg to a hen.
He's not just a little fling,
He's my everything!

9. Occupations

I love you
and there's too many ways to say it!
I love you
and if I was a musician,
I would write a song and play it,
In front of a huge crowd,
they would be screaming so loud,
my ears would burst!
I love you
and if I was an artist,
I would paint a picture and hang it on a
wall.
Pray to God that the nail is strong enough,
so it won't fall!
I love you.
And, if I was a football player,
I would tackle everybody that hurt you,
and score a touchdown, for your heart!
I love you.
And, if I was a dancer,
I would dance circles around the girls that
try and take my spot,
making them dizzy until they drop!

I love you.
And, if I was the president,
I would make you my 1st man
and together no one could stop us,
unless they shot us,
of course!
I love you.
And, if I was a builder,
I would mend your broken heart,
with the cement of love!
I love you.
And, if I was a writer,
I would write books and poems about our
love.
This is the best way to show you that
I love you!

10. The First Year

1 year of pure love.
1 year of pure joy.
1 year of lost girl.
1 year of confused boy.
1 year ago, they met.
1 year ago, they fell in love.

It started off great.
Then, went from bad to worse.
They didn't know how
they were gonna break this curse!

Then one day, the truth finally came out.
He told her how
he had been stepping out!

It broke her heart
and tore her apart.
She wasn't sure
if they could make a fresh start.

He begged and pleaded,
swore he would change.

She forgave him and said they'd work it out
But she didn't know if they're relationship
would ever be the same.

They talked,
but it wasn't like before.
She didn't know if she could take it anymore!
She wanted it back to the way it was.
When they were happy and all in love!
Then, one day it all just changed.
He became sweeter, nicer, and a range of
things.
It's like she fell in love all over again!

They have bad times
As all relationships do
But
they always seemed to work it out.
Because, that's what being together is all
about!
Ok, enough of this "he" and "she",
The rest of this poem is coming straight
from me.
Baby, I love you more than you know
I pray to God you never let me go.

I want to be with you for much longer.
I hope our relationship will grow stronger.
The times we share are the best of my life.
I hope one day you'll make me your wife.
I want to be together for a long time, you
see.

I just want to be part of your sweet, sweet
family!

Together forever, I love you, it's true
1-year isn't enough time of being with you!

11. Good Days

I love you.
Since day one, butterflies flourished under
the sun.
Day two, I want it to be just me and you.
Day three, dreams of a proposal on one knee.
Day four, I search no more.
Day five, I finally feel alive.
Day six, my shattered heart is now fixed.
Day seven, God sculpted you for me, from
heaven.
Day eight, my heart runs with love that
won't dissipate.
Day nine, the stars have fallen in line.
Day ten, I knew you were my ticket to
falling in love again.
I love you!

12. Bad Days

I hate you.
Since day one, I knew we were done.
Day two, my heart resented you.
Day three, the sight of you kills me.
Day four, my soul can't take no more.
Day five, no more tears for your lies.
Day six, bones and sticks, words can't fix.
Day seven, you used my insecurities as a
weapon.
Day eight, I hate… I hate… I hate…
Day nine, …………..
Day ten, you're dead to me, all is well then.
I hate you!

13. All Mine

Baby I love you!
You're my one and only Boo.
The one I wanna give my all to.
The one I have dreams of being with forever.
I hate it whenever
you leave my side.
Makes me want to run and hide,
until I see you
the next time.

14. I Want to Be

I don't want to have a place in your heart,
I want to be it.
I want to be your heart AND your soul.
The one you crave when you're away,
The one you hold tight when you're close.
I want you to yearn for my body,
yearn for my touch.
I want to be the one you're afraid to lose,
I want to be your one,
your one and only.

15. Why?

I don't know why I love him so much.
Why he makes my heart melt.
Why it skips a beat whenever he's near.
Why my hands get so sweaty,
my stomach starts to churn,
a cat has my tongue.
I don't know why I love him so much.
Why his hugs heal the aching in my heart
Why his kisses...
God, his kisses!
Enough said.

16. Yearning Desires

I wish I loved him as much as I love you.
I wish I yearned to see him smile,
yearned to hear his laugh
yearned to be held in his arms as much as I
yearn for you.
I wish the joy I get when I see you, could be
transferred to him.
I wish my heart leapt out my chest when I
think of him, just as I of you.
I wish the thought of him giving his love to
another, crushed my heart into a million
pieces,
only you have that power.
I wish more than anything that he were you.

17. Dreaming

Dreams of our future together,
I wish you were here
Caressing my hair,
holding me tight as I sleep.

18. I Would Like

I would like to walk down the street,
have somebody say,
"Hey, that's her!"
I would like to have a lot of friends,
to feel like I belong,
like I could do or say anything
and it would be okay.
I would like to be loved for who I am and
not for what I have.
To be the one everybody looks up to.
I would like to not be shy anymore.
And for once in my life,
I would like to be noticed!

19. Dear Uncle Mac,

It's been 7 days since you left this world.
Life isn't going too good
I wish that I could
be up there with you right now.
It seems like when you left,
everything was turned upside down,
stepped on and pushed all the way in the
ground.
Why couldn't you stay?
Why did you have to pass away
that day?
It wasn't fair.
He took you too soon.
You weren't supposed to go beyond the moon.
You were supposed to stay here with me.
You remember when you used to get those
scratch offs
and
we would sit in your car
and
eat snacks
while you scratched?
I would be over your shoulder,

seeing if you won,
It used to be so much fun.
I will remember that for eternity.
I miss you so much.
I will always be your "Kaylam."
Save a place for me in heaven!
I love you!
-Kaylam

20. Anxiety

Legs shaking uncontrollably,
stomach making weird noises,
head spinning.
Small yellow pills.
Visits to the doctor.
Getting a pass.
Leaving class,
Anxious,
sitting in the conference room,
wondering,
if it's going to end soon.
Staying up, crying half the night away.
Having thoughts about stabbing my heart
away.
Going off on someone who was just trying to
take the pain away.
Who am I?
Anxiety.
And, I'm no joke!

21. Look

Nobody sees that she's slowly drifting away.
Look into her eyes.
You'll see all the hurt and pain,
the suffering and the shame.
You'll see her heart;
Decaying rose petals
onto the floor!
But nobody sees her.
She's invisible.

22. Deep Within

If you look deep into my eyes,
right past my heart,
you'll see my soul.
Rocking back and forth in a corner,
screaming,
"I wanna die!
I wanna fly high!
I wanna go somewhere where I'm free!
Free to just be me.

23. Scars of the Past

Loving you is hard.
After all the other scars,
I just can't seem to shake off the hurt and
pain.
The regret and the shame.
I know this may sound lame,
but
it's how I feel.
And if I get it off my chest,
my heart may heal.
They hurt me, and I can't forgive.
Some days I don't even want to live,
I want to curl up in a ball and die.
Just want to lie,
in the ground and rot
in the spot
they made for me.
I just want to be put out of my misery.
I don't want to live this life anymore,
I want to be the person I was before.
Carefree and kind.
Silly girl with an innocent mind,
not these evil emotions like jealousy and
hate.

I just want to be the old me.
I want my heart and soul to be free
Forgive, Forget, and just be me!
But
they broke me.

24. Don't Love Myself

How can I LOVE someone,
when I can't even LOVE myself?
Stay up all night thinking,
why can't I love me?
What's wrong with me?
How can someone like me,
when I don't even like myself?
I hate my body.
My stomach.
My clothes.
My hair.
My nose.
My fingers.
My toes.
My laugh.
My cry.
My hello.
My goodbye.
My EVERYTHING!

25. Dreamland

Lonely days.
Sleepless nights.
Tears streaming down my face.
Heart heavy,
broken in two.
Hard to breathe.
Can't think straight.
Going down a dark tunnel,
seeing the light.
Walking closer
BAM!
Hit by a semi-
Feeling life go
Goodbye!
SPLASH!
Water on my face.
It was all a dream.

26. Un-Real

Un-loved.
Un-appreciated.
That's how I feel!
Life is so un-real!
Un-friendly
Un-likeable
That's how I feel!
Life feels so
un-real!
I can't tell anyone about this thing,
I ain't talking,
I'm keeping it in!
I won't even tell my best friend!
I can't tell her about this.
I'm too ashamed,
to speak on this forbidden thing!
So, I'm suffering in silence.
Un-approachable,
un-known.
That's how I feel!
Life is so
un-real!

27. Torture

The pain I feel inside is indescribable,
unbearable.
I don't know what's the cause
I don't know what's the solution.
I'm tired.
Tired of being strong.
Tired of holding on.
Tired of it all.
There are no tears,
yet plenty of fears,
Holding me back from life.
The pain I feel is torture;
sweet, sweet torture.

28. Defeat

I don't know what I want.
Confused.
Sad.
Hurt.
Upset.
Defeated.
I wish life was so much easier than it is.
I just want to be happy.

29. Questioning

Feeling like the world is coming down on my
head.
Laying in my bed,
thinking about how I wish things could be.
Me being hella happy,
not worrying about all the drama in life.
Feels like I must sacrifice
everything to make other people happy.
But, what about me?
Who's going to help me?
Who's going to sacrifice for me?
Who?

30. Boring Class (5th per. AP English)

Sitting in this boring ass class.
Watching the time go past.
Staring at the clock
hearing it, "tick-tock",
Slowly around the frame the hands go,
slow,
so slow,
the hands go!
Hurry up bell and ring,
sing
that sweet song,
so, I can move along
to the next class.
But, slowly,
so slowly,
the hands go past,
having me trapped in this boring ass class!

31. Paper, Pen, Poetry

I haven't written in a while.
Nothing has inspired me, I guess it's
time to put the paper and pen to rest,
move on to other things.
But I just can't forget about my 1st love,
The one who knows about my hurt, my pain,
my loss, my gain.
The one who helped me through thick and thin,
when I needed a friend
to just sit and listen.
Not criticize and judge,
or push me when I didn't want to budge.
Life is getting hectic,
I can't take it.
I need you in my life
so, I can survive,
stay alive.
Revive
the old me.
Kill
the new me.
Go back to being happy
not feeling crappy.
I just want to be me.

Let this demon free!
It's crazy how much I've changed,
I'm not the same.
So, I need you,
to keep me sane.
You're all I have,
Paper, Pen, Poetry.

32. Why Do You Treat Me This Way?

Why do we always fight?
It seems like everything I say just ain't right.
You hang up the phone in my ear,
bringing up a little tear.
You say you love me,
I say I love you, too.
But
how would you feel if I did that to you?
I want you,
you want me, too
Apparently not if I'm going through
all this pain,
because of you.
You treat me like dirt
Don't you know that really hurts?
I love you more than life or death.
But I think I gotta get with someone else.
You want me to be your baby
I want you to be my man
But there's one thing that you just don't seem to
understand...
I have feelings just like you.
when you do this to me, I start to hate you.

If you keep doing me like this,
I might have to find
a boy unlike you,
Who loves me enough to never, ever turn me blue.

33. Playing Games

Occasionally,
a good man comes in your life.
Then the next thing you know he's gone,
just like that,
Comes in, gone and ain't coming back.
He comes in but,
he doesn't stay.
He comes in and he just plays.
Plays with your heart, your mind,
making you think everything would be just
fine.
He comes in and plays games.
He comes in and says things
that will make you melt.
He comes in and messes with your head,
you're stuck wondering why you're being led
down this path of hurt and deceit.
You think to yourself, "I can do better."
But, better never comes.
You stay longer than you intended to.
You can't let go because you love him too
much.
You wish he would stay
instead of coming in to play!

34. I Need Answers

I'm in love with a boy who doesn't love me.
I think about him all the time.
Can't gather up enough courage to tell him
how I feel.
What if he doesn't feel the same way?
I'd be crushed.
This would be another time
where I've fallen for a boy who doesn't like
me.
I want someone who will love me
unconditionally.
I need someone to love me for me.
I just can't seem to find anyone like that
I'm always falling for little boys.
Ones who don't know how to treat a woman.
I'm tired of them messing with my heart,
doing everything in their power to make me
feel unworthy.
I'm tired of getting hurt.
Tired of crying myself to sleep every night.
I'm tired of being tired.
When will I find the one for me?

35. Are You for Me?

When you say, "I love you," do you really
mean it?
Is it just something you say because it
sounds right?
Does it have any meaning to you?
Well, to me it does.
It means that you care,
you'll be fair,
and you'll respect my wishes.
We'll share little kisses
from time to time.
We'll hold hands,
let everybody know you're my man.
My sexy dark chocolate.
Someone I can kick it with.
Someone I can call my own.
Someone I can be alone
with.
But, are you for me?
Do you even want to be?

36. God's Plan or devil's work

God,
is this Your plan?
Is this Your way of telling me him and I
shouldn't be?
Is this Your way of telling me that he's not
worthy of me?
Are You telling me that this boy will end up
hurting me
eventually?
That he won't love me unconditionally?
God,
is this Your way of telling me
that even though he seems like the perfect
man,
he's actually a dog?
Or
Is this the devil's work
trying to make me THINK that I don't need him?
Trying to force me to THINK that we won't fall
in love?
Trying to make me THINK that he will be just
like those other boys?
I don't know what to believe.

37. This Feeling

I got this feeling...
It won't go away!
I got this feeling.
I think it's going to stay!
I got this feeling...
He's cheating!

38. I Know

I know he's cheating on me.
I can feel it in my bones.
He says he's not,
but he's lying like stones!

39. Rage

Every time I see you with that girl,
it makes me want to hurl.
I hope she comes down with a deadly disease,
one that will have her on her knees,
begging God,
"Help me, help me, PLEASE!

Love and Luv
is <u>NOT</u>
the same thing! -A.Q.

40. I'm Sorry

I'm sorry that you hurt me.
I'm sorry that you lied to me.
I'm sorry that you cheated on me.
I'm sorry that you made me hate you.
I'm sorry that you made me cry myself to
sleep most nights.
I'm sorry that you dropped my heart and
watched it shatter.
I'm sorry that she made you leave me.
I'm sorry that you listened to him instead of
your heart.
I'm sorry that you're insecure and accused me
of cheating.
I'm sorry that you made me not trust you.
I'm sorry that you didn't really love me.
I'm sorry that you were an asshole to me.
I'm sorry that I came into your life.
I'm sorry that you're a sorry excuse for a
man,
I'm sorry that you're not man enough to even
apologize to me!

41. Dear You

Dear You,
I'm just going to come out and say it:
Fuck you!
Fuck you, fuck you, fuck you!
What the hell is your problem?
Don't you want to be with me?
You told me yeah.
But, you ain't doing nothing about it!
So, you know what:
Just forget it!
Don't worry about me!
You don't care and that shit hurts!
So, fuck it!
AND
FUCK
YOU!

42. Care

You don't care,
So why should I?
We wanna be together but
you don't even try!
I'm trying to work this out
But why?
How are we going to do this if you aren't
trying?
I love you and you obviously don't care!
Why is that?
Don't you think about me all day, every day?
Don't you wish I was with you all the time?
Don't you want to hold me in your "big" arms?
Don't you luv me?

43. Boy!

What's wrong with you?
You always say nothing.
But it's got to be something!
You're not your old goofy self.
It's like you took that part out and put it
on a high shelf!
You don't say sweet things like you used to.
You don't call me Baby or Boo.
You barely say I love you!
We don't talk.
It's like we barely know each other.
I miss the old you.
The one who used to say, "Hey bae"
and called me every day!
I miss the you who used to make me laugh.
The one that was like my other half!
The new one makes me cry and feel bad,
he makes me happy
only when he's not mad.
PLEASE bring the old you back!

44. Make Up Your Mind!

Are we together?
Yes or no?
Should I keep holding on,
Or should I let go?
Boy I keep giving my heart to you
And all you do
Is break it!
I can't take it
Anymore!
I can't live my life for you,
I have to live it for me
And that's how it's forever going to be!

45. Decision to be Made

Confused on who to choose.
Confused on who I wanna lose.
I love them both,
But who do I love the most?

46. Wait

A month.
No kiss.
Two months,
nothing yet.
Three months
and still nothing!
Could you wait that long?
Just to get a taste of something that's
probably not that good.
Could you wait a year?
Two years?
If I wanted to have sex.
Wanted to give you the only precious thing I
have left?
Could you wait for the day that I say, 'I love
you'?
Or, would you rush me,
Punch, slap, hit, kick me
until you got what you wanted?
Would you really hurt me like that?
Really make me feel like shit just to please
yourself?
At first, I thought you were different,
now I see I might be wrong!

47. Free to be Me!

Sitting here thinking about the past,
wondering why I was always last
on your list.
You claimed you loved me,
yet, you treated me wrong.
Thought I would be there when all those
other girls were gone.
Guess I was wrong.

But I'm not living my life for you
anymore.
I gotta do what I gotta do
for me
to be happy.
If that means never speaking to you again,
then by all means,
that's what I'm going to do!

It's time for me to let you go!
To be free.
To be me.
Without you!

48. A Letter to The Boy I Loved the Most

Dear Most Loved,
The way you look at me, I know you still
want me.
You're just scared that your girlfriend will
find out.
I know you lied to me when you said I was
your 1st love,
I don't know why I fell for it.
The truth is I did love you, more than I let
you believe.
However,
I never said anything because I didn't feel
loved back.
My feelings were right though,
You didn't love me like you said you did.
You were playing me from the beginning,
I was just stupid and didn't catch it until
it was too late,
until I got a broken heart.
Yeah, I know I told you I just want to be
friends,
that we were too different.

I was just agreeing with you
so, it didn't seem like I was being a brat,
so, I didn't get on your nerves.
Why did you do it?
Why did you trick me and everybody else to
make us think that you really liked me?
That you "loved" me?
Why did I have to be your victim?
I thought I was your baby, your boo 'til the
end?
This wasn't fair.
You were messing with my emotions.
I loved you and I still do,
so why did you do me like that?
Why did you play me?
Why did you treat me like a princess,
Only to do me like dirt?
What happened between us?
It seemed like we just gave up,
like we didn't even care.
Or,
were you trying to reunite with your
homegirl,
so, it didn't matter to you anyway?
You used to look at me, like I was the only
thing you would never let go of,
like we were going to be together forever.
Like, we were going to be the perfect couple-
at least close to it.
Looks can be deceiving.
I can't blame everything on you,
it was partly my fault, too.

I wasn't communicating,
I wouldn't let you in.
I just didn't trust another boy to come into
my heart.
I thought you would break it-
you did.
I tried to prevent myself from acting that
way with you.
I tried to open up.
I was afraid to trust.
I was afraid to love!
Baby I'm sorry
for treating you like I didn't care.
Well, Boo, I really did and do love you.
I miss you so much
and I hope you have a great life with or
without me in it!
Love,
Me

49. Crashing

Feeling like the world is coming down on my
head.
Wish I could lay in bed
and pretend to be dead.
My head is spinning,
my legs are weak.
My heart is filled with hate,
hate in which I can't speak.
I can't let it out,
I don't know how.
Who I can run to?
Who can I tell this about?
Who would be willing to listen?
To experience my pain?
Pain in which I can't see,
pain in which I can't dream,
pain in which I can't be me.
Just pain.

50. Knife

I could never drive that knife thru my
heart.
Images of my parents, tore me apart
crying and pleading
wondering why,
why their only child chose to die?
Pictures of mommy falling to her knees,
Daddy trying to hold her up, begging God
please!
"Please bring my baby back to me!"
I don't want to put them through such pain,
so, I suffer in silence, much to my disdain.
I suffer so I won't break anyone's heart,
even though mine is torn apart.
Tired of being strong
tired of holding on
tired of it all!
When will it end?
This feeling in my chest,
no matter what I do,
nothing feels like my best.
I can't get anything right,
no matter how much I fight.

Can't get these thoughts out of my head.
Thoughts of wanting to be dead.
Thoughts of ending it all right now,
thoughts of figuring out how,
I would take my own life.
But I can't act on these thoughts.
I can't fall.
I must remain strong
for everyone.
But
who's going to be there for me when I am
weak?

51. Eggshells

It's exhausting trying to be the peace in my
parent's storm.
The constant arguing.
Going back and forth.
Loud.
Slamming doors.
Silence for days.
Just make it stop.
Walking on eggshells.
Don't know if tonight will be good or bad,
so, I wait.
Holding my breath as the keys jingle in the
door.
Will it be, "Hello." Or "Hey babies!"
...
"Hey babies!"
I exhale.
Tonight, will be a good night.
But, how long will it last?

52. Neglect

Do you love me?
Can you hear me?
Am I invisible?
I need you.
Why are you ignoring me?
Am I not worthy?
Mommy? Hello?
Daddy don't go!
Don't walk out that door!
Your job can wait!
Do you notice me?
Alone in my room.
Nobody to turn to.
Not even you!
Don't even know what I'm up to.
You say you love me,
I don't see it,
you don't mean it.
Do I have to call you on the phone to get
your attention?
Help you build a house so we can build a
bond?
You don't hear me.

Can't see me.
I'm invisible to you.
Neglect.

Can't see me.
I'm invisible to you.

53. Kicked Out

Heard a bunch of yelling and banging coming
from down the hall.
Running so fast, I thought I might fall.
Saw mommy standing on top of the bed,
Daddy trying to tip it over,
looking like he wanted Mommy dead.
At first it looked like a game.
I asked if everything was okay,
They say,
"Yes."
I walk back to my room,
frightened.
Worried.
More yelling.
I scream for them to shut up!
Please, just shut up!
They didn't hear me.
Next thing I know
Mommy is being pushed out of the door.
Daddy said,
"She's not welcomed here anymore."
I scream and I plead,

"Please let Mommy stay with me!"
But my pleading goes upon deaf ears.
Mommy had to drive away from here.
Leaving me behind.

54. Back to Love

We've been through a lot,
these past few days.
Trying to find our way
back to the beginning.
Where love was new,
fresh.
Now,
it's full of stress,
pain,
Before, it was sparks, now it's just...
Plain.

55. Pieces

Why can't I get over you?
All the stuff you say and do,
I should be over you
but I can't.
You got a hold on me
that can't break free.
You got me sitting in my room dazed
while you're out all night getting blazed.
I sit and wonder what life would have been
like if I was still with you.
I'd probably be the happiest I've ever been!
But...
Is that with the old you or the new?
The one who always knew what to say to
make me laugh?
Or, the one who knows what to say to make me
cry?
The one who knew all of me?
Or, the one who uses that knowledge against
me?
The one who said we'd be together forever
and always?
Or, the one who got my hopes up, then

smashed them back down?
The one who I've loved from the first time we
talked?
Or, the one I've despised since he first re-
opened that door to my heart?
Why can't I let the old you go?
Why do I keep putting myself in a place
where I know I'm going to get hurt?
When I know the old you is never coming
back!
He is gone and, in his place, he left a
heartless piece of…
Piece of…
A **piece** of a man who has been through a lot
in life.
Who has been hurt by people he never
expected to get hurt by.
Who has lost those who were very close to
him.
A **piece** of a man that I want to hold in my
arms until all his problems go away.
A man I'm learning to love.
A man I want to spend the rest of my life
with.
But that won't happen,
it can't.
Because, all I'll try to do is get the old you
back.
But he's gone.
Forever and always.

56. Senses

Sounds like the shattering of glass.
Feels like an atomic bomb
exploding in your chest.
Looks like a wilted flower,
its life slowly slipping away, then taken
all at once.
Tastes like raw apricot seeds,
crunchy and delicious at first,
then gradually sour and bitter,
choking you.
Smells like a decaying body,
rancid, horrid.
The 5 senses of a broken heart.

57. Moving On

Moving on is hard
when you're stuck in the past,
stuck in a realm of what ifs,
how comes,
and why didn't it last?
Stuck in the hurt,
stuck in the pain,
driving you insane.
Moving on is hard
when you're still stuck on the 1st,
1st hug,
1st kiss,
1st heartache,
1st diss,
1st time crying yourself to sleep,
with a knife clenched in your fist.
Moving on is hard,
But, seeing them with someone else is even
harder.
Holding hands,
laughing together,
kissing each other,
seeing the love that once belonged to you,

fade into oblivion.
Given to another
like it was theirs all along.
Who is now the mother,
of the child that was supposed to be ours.
While you're lying in bed
crying to slow songs
moving on is hard,
But, eventually it will all get better.

58. I Miss

I miss the feeling of loving you.
The pounding in my heart when you are near.
The butterflies in my stomach with just the
thought of you.
I miss the feeling of needing you.
Needing the touch of your hand,
the smell of your cologne,
the love in your eyes.
I miss you.

59. Remembrance

Trying to get over you is hard to do.
When everything I look at reminds me of you.
Every time I turn on the radio, I hear our
song.
Remembering you and I holding hands,
singing along.

60. Hurt

You gave your love to someone else.
You shared your body with another.
You made a life with some other.
My love for you was supposed to wash away
the pain,
but it remains.
I'm hurting more
than ever before
but I must be strong.
I must let go and I must move on.
Let go of this hurt
Move on from the pain,
find my rainbow
in all this rain.
I must let go of the betrayal.
Move on from the broken heart,
let go of the promise we made from the start.

61. No Longer

I no longer feel that ache in my heart.
Or care about what you do,
or who you do it with.
I no longer yearn for you.
So, have I finally moved on?
Or, have I masked the pain so well,
I can't feel it anymore?

62. Hello Friend

Hello friend,
here I am again.
Alone with my mind.
Hoping to find
a solution to all the madness.
Wishing you could help
But, you can't,
'cause I'm a lost cause.
So, while you're moving on,
with the one you're supposed to be with
I'll be weeping in secret,
but, smile in your face.
I love you with so much passion.
It wraps me in its arms and warms me like a
blanket,
it's too much!
I must end it all!
So, the pain of loving you can be
transferred to someone new!
I love you
'til my dying breath.

63. Obsession

I hate how I get when you say you love me.
The constant butterflies.
The warm fuzzy feeling.
The thoughts of the future.
The love I have for you is too much.
Cross my heart,
hope to die,
stick a needle in my eye.
My heart bleeds for you,
dying to be close to you,
too blind to stay away from you.
Hate how clingy I get when you say you'll
never leave me.
Grab onto your pants leg and drag me across
the floor,
mopping up the pain of not having you,
the tears I cry for you.
I love you too much, but
you say that's not possible.
You could never feel this.
If you were cold,
I'd split myself in half, wrap myself around
you,
will my heart to keep pumping so you can be

warm.
If you were hurting,
I'd grab the pain out of your body and put it
inside of me,
so, you'd be free.
If you died,
I would beg God to trade places with you,
"Take me instead. So, he can live on!"
I love you too much.
I can't sleep, breathe, think, survive without
you.
I love you too much.
It hurts!
Too clingy, too attached, too obsessed.
Lock me up.
I'm going insane!
I can't do this anymore...
I'm afraid.

64. What If

As I lay in bed, I think of the what ifs.
What if we had…?
What if we had not…?
But it doesn't matter.
It's never going to happen.
So, as I twirl this knife into my chest,
I take the possibility of finding the what
ifs, with me.
I leave you to wonder
As I slip into the fire…
Goodbye.

65. Best Friend

I lost my best friend,
my right hand,
the one I could confide in.
I lost my go-to,
the one I could run to
who always knew
what to say to turn my gray skies blue.
I lost my better half,
the one that always made me laugh,
until tears streamed down my face.
I lost my favorite shoulder.
The one I could lean on in my time of
despair.
I lost...

66. Oxygen

The tears rolling down my face
is the pain I feel of not being near you.
My chest hurts because my heart is breaking.
I can't breathe because you are my oxygen,
and you're nowhere to be found.

67. Empty Vessel

I thought you were my heart and soul.
But you left me
just skin and bones.
An empty vessel.

68. You Left Me

I needed you and you left me…
You left me in the dark…
You were my light and you left me…

69. Toy Story

You put me on a shelf, Andy
Waiting to be picked up and loved again.
Return to being your best friend, Andy.

You left me with the others, Andy
I was supposed to be your one and only,
but you treated me like a dusty, old toy,
Andy.

You chose others over me, Andy
Picked them up and treated them better.
You've got a friend in me,
but you couldn't see.
Our love dropped to the floor
when you walked through the door
leading to you walking over me, Andy.

I was your Woody,
then came Buzz
replacing what was once just us.

You put me in a box, Andy
Turned your back on me,

I tried to escape and run after you,
it was too late.
You didn't want me anymore,
Gave me to someone else,
I'm going to miss you, Andy.
So long, partner.

70. Apologies

I made you my counselor; you weren't
equipped with that degree.

Made you my little secret, hidden from the
world, only known by me.

Made you my punching bag, taking my anger
out on you.

Made you angry and upset, emotions you
shouldn't have to feel from someone who loves
so much of you.

Made you taste me badly, looking at me in a
negative light.

Made you stop talking to me, your silence
only death could defy.

I made you stop loving me, pushed the most
important person out of my life.

I'm sorry.

71. Tame

Hopefully, she can tame that beast inside of
you,
an achievement I couldn't do.
You wouldn't allow me to
get too close to you,
You didn't trust me.
You kept distance between you and me,
but I'd travel across any sea
to close that gap between.
Even if only as a friend
because in the end,
I fell in love with that beast inside of you.
So, hopefully she can be what you need
since you wouldn't allow me to be,
your tamer.

72. Why Won't You Just Roll Up the Window?

The sun is so hot,
it's boiling my skin,
but I literally want to feel the rage I have
within.

73. Flare

You're no good for me.
You spark my anxiety.
Make it hard to breathe.
Take the wind right out of me.
Before I go to sleep.
You're my last thought.
My only dream.
That's too much for me,
you have my anxiety
going haywire.

74. Temple

My body is a temple.
I will NOT let you into.
You're not worthy of my precious jewel.
Can't just have your way with me.
I'm not Burger King.
You were once my king,
my happily ever after
'til I found out it was only my goodies you
were after.
Now you're the evil villain.
Make life hard to live in.
I won't let you steal it away from me,
I've decided to break free
from your grasp,
give this ass
to someone more deserving
of a Queen like me.

75. Away

I missed you.
But, the thoughts in my head almost killed
me.
Had to stay away from the world.
Get my head on straight
so, I wouldn't go thru those fiery gates.
Was in a mental hell.
So, I had to clear my mind.
Needed time.
To think things through.
Had to get away from it all,
including you.

76. I Give You Away

Used to love you as much as the sun loved the
sky,
brightly!
Realized the attraction was only sexual,
started to hate you,
strongly.
Trying to keep my mind off the pain my heart is
feeling,
the constant lies,
"She's just a friend."
"Don't believe everything you hear or see."
"I love you."
I still went against the grain and stood by you,
only for you to throw HER in my face.
You got headaches, huh?
I was supposed to be your medicine,
but you treated me like spoiled food.
Like I'm the one that ruined you.
You brought this upon yourself,
got yourself in this mess.
Hopefully, SHE can help you out of it.
I'm done.

77. Inconsistent

You were the only constant thing in my life.
Then, you left.

78. Give It Back

Nights like this,
I reminisce.
When we shared a kiss
or
almost had your chocolate stick between my
lips,
coating it with my spit,
shit woulda been lit!
But it never happened.
It never will.
You love her.
You need her.
She's everything I'm not
for you.
My love for you is so intense,
that I have none left to give
to anyone else,
not even myself!
You stole that from me
so, I'm asking for it back.
Please!

79. Cold Hearted

You turned my heart cold
that's a bold
move for someone who was supposed to love
me.
But, you didn't.
You kept me around because I was a puppy.
I ran to you, jumped up and down to be
noticed by you.
No matter how many times you pushed me
away,
I came running back.
Thinking it was a game,
a fun way of showing me you loved me,
I didn't feel the pain
of being rejected.
The hurt of being pushed aside.
All I felt was love.
A heart burning with infinite love.
Then one day I grew up,
became a full-grown dog,
you pushed me away one too many times.
I won't be running back.

80. I HATE YOU!

I hate you!
I hate how much I need you,
need you to be there for me.
I hate how much I want you,
want you to hold me.
I hate how much I love you,
with every fiber of my being!
I hate how much the thoughts of you float
into my day to day,
float into my dreams!
I hate how much you've taken away from me,
every bit of my energy,
I'm drained!
I hate how much you affect me.
I can't function!
I love you so much that I hate you!
and I don't know how to make it stop!

81. Breathless

I used to love you so passionately,
it scared me.
Made my breath
catch in my chest,
made it hard to breathe.

82. This Is the Hard Part

Why is letting you go so hard?
We've had our time.
It didn't work,
but it still hurts!
Loving you hurts,
I must love the pain,
the torture of it all.

83. Suffering

Suffering at the hands of the one who said
he loved me like no other.
Said his love was my last and greatest,
the last one to love me like he does.
Said he couldn't stop loving me even if he
tried,

      he stopped.
Said the last thing he wanted to do was
cause me pain,
  yet,

       he did.
The pain is suffocating, hard to breathe,
      I love it!
Love the pain he's caused me,
can't stay away.
He is a piece of me.

He said I was enough,
but he didn't value me.
Said he wanted me happy,
but he is my happiness!
He keeps me alive!
Said he didn't get the kind of love & care I

provide.
I'm the only one who made him feel this way.
Said he was my protector
     I don't feel safe.
I feel left in this place,
as he goes on protecting her.
Giving her my knight in shining armor.
Said I hold half his heart,
     it's not enough.
I want it all!
I want to be his soul.
All he wants,
    Needs
but it can't be.
He doesn't need me.
So,
   I suffer.

84. Board Game

You got a hold on me,
can't break free.
Play me like Monopoly.
I'm in jail,
$200 bail
I can't afford.
So, I'm stuck
in this hell,
in this cell,
trapped!
Can't move my piece around the board
to get away from you,
So, I'm living on the streets.
No place to call my own
you took every property away from me.
You win.

85. Mind Dump

You broke me.
I'm broken
IT HURTS!
Heart ripped out of my chest
stomped on!
Lie after lie after lie after lie after lie
after lie after lie after lie after lie!
Pushed me away when I was trying to love
you.
You chose others over me.
Picked me up when it was convenient.
Dropped me off at the bus stop,
never taking that route again.
If you love her like you say you do,
why keep me around?
I'm not a toy!
You can't pick me up & put me down
whenever you're bored!
I have feelings!
I have a heart,
that used to only beat for you,
but now it sings a different tune!
I would have loved you more than she ever

could!
Hell, I already do!
I love you with every blink of an eye,
every beat of a heart,
every breath, in and out,
every nervous tick,
every head itch,
every racing thought.
I want it all to stop!

86. High Horse

What are these wet things falling from my
eyes?
Is it your many lies?
The pain you've caused?
Exhaustion?
Broken promises?
Taken my love as one of your tokens?
Is it just lack of sleep?
All the muddied dreams getting to me?
Making up things that I want to believe?
Could you truly be bad for me?
I just didn't want to see?
So, instead I put you on a pedestal?
It's time for you to come down now.

87. Every

I'm starting to have dreams of you.
Every emotion
flooding back to me.
Every memory
clashing like a symphony.
Every hug
taking ahold of me.
Every laugh
a perfect harmony.
Limited kisses
shared between
you and me.

88. Home

Want to feel the softness of your lips brush
against mine.
Your fingertips running down my spine.
See the love in your eyes.
Feel the home in your arms.

89. Exploration

Come inside me.
Explore.
Taste my thoughts.
Hit the G-spot
in my heart
where only you can touch.
Explore my walls.
Read the calligraphy of my past,
don't judge me.
Caress my emotions until they burst.
Let them spill into your hands
hold on tight,
don't play with them!
Smell my pain.
Fill your lungs with the sweet torture.
Exhale.
Hear my cries,
pleasure and pain.
eardrums combust,
explosion of extasy.
Come inside of me-
Stay forever.

90. Wanting You

I want to be in your arms.
Kiss your lips, softly.
Feel the electricity rush through my body.
I want to hear your heartbeat.
Look into your eyes and see the love I've
been craving.
I want you.
Now.
Forever.
Always.

91. Sanity

I want to be your sanity.
The one that keeps you sane.
I want to be the whole of you,
the one you can contain.

92. Organs

I don't just love you,
I yearn you,
I need you,
I can't be without you,
I want to be in you,
surrounded by the warmth of your flesh.
Play guitar with your tendons.
Jump on your stomach like a trampoline.
Use your veins like a swing.
Use your windpipe like a pole
and scroll
down to your heart
listen to it beat,
my favorite melody.

93. Because of You

How can you get through
days without me?
But I need you, see
you're the reason I'm still alive.
Saved me many nights
from leaving this world, forever.
I never
thought I'd see this day,
live to be this age.
But, because of you
it's possible.
Because of you
I'm able to love you longer.
Because of you,
I am.

94. Completion

I love you the long way,
the hard way.
I love you more than God,
who gave His only Son.
You are my sun.
Brighten up my darkest days,
warm my soul,
make me whole.
I'm complete when you're near.

95. Smack

You are my addiction,
my drug,
take a needle to my arm
fill me up.
Get high off you,
dazed.
blazed.
After one sniff,
high off your love.
Head in the clouds,
looking from above.
Roll you up,
spark it up,
and inhale you.
You're inside of me,
until my next fix.

96. Muse

You are my muse.
My motivation.
My inspiration.
The reason for my flow,
you helped create it.
Helped mold me,
guide me,
to be a better me.
Helped build me up,
filled me
with encouragement,
love,
positivity.
You saved me.
Gave me strength.
You are my perfect piece of art.

97. Invasion

When I think of you,
my chest tightens,
my heart is attacking itself,
trying to get back to you.
I think about your touch,
my body catches fire!
The sound of your voice,
slightly becoming a distant memory,
still shakes me to my core!
Your smile
invades my mind, 25/8!
I miss you so much
It feels like my life is falling apart
without you in it.
I need you to breathe,
you fill my lungs!
I need you to survive,
You are my strength!
I need you to love me,
You are my life!
But I must let all that go.
Try and go on without relying on you.
Some days, I'm okay.
Other days, I feel like tracking you down,
kidnapping you and driving far, far away.
Just you and me.

98. Painful Bliss

I'm in love with the pain that you cause.

99. Quote

"It only takes one right turn to make up for
all the wrong turns in your life."

100. Acceptance

What's the point of changing my ways,
if everyone's just going to view me the same?
Why does she have an attitude?
I'm literally just sitting here.
Why is she so sarcastic?
That's just my personality. I'm only joking!
Why is she making that facial expression?
It's literally just my face.
Why is she laughing, it wasn't even that
funny?
I have Social Anxiety, it's a nervous tick,
sorry.
Now it's my turn.
Why can't y'all just accept me for me?

101. LISTEN!

Listen to me!
Turn off your mind and hear me!
Mute your judgement.
Pay attention to the words coming out of my
mouth!
I'VE CHANGED!
I'M NOT THE SAME!
GET ME OUT OF THAT BUBBLE!
My attitude has improved.
I'm not who you're used
to.
Stop assuming things about me,
just ask.
I'll tell you everything you need to know.
If I say I've moved on,
believe me,
I'm not trying to be stuck in the past.
YOU won't let it go!
STOP JUDGING ME AND JUST LISTEN!
Please!

102. Swarming Thoughts

I can't sleep.
Mind clouded in heaps,
piles of unresolved shit,
I can't handle it.

103. Dancing with the devil

I suffer in silence,
So, no one worries,
worries about me feeling alone in a room
full of people.
People don't seem to notice.
Notice a smile on my face but, I'm dying on
the inside.
Inside by soul wants to hide.
Hide in a ditch.
A ditch so deep it covers my feet,
6 feet.
6 feet deep is where I want to be,
to be free.
Free from all this pain.
This pain inside my head.
My head is going to explode.
Explode of all brain matter.
That's all that matters
That matters is the pain will be gone.
Gone.
Gone.
Gone.
I have no one to talk to.
To talk to about this stuff.
This stuff going on in my life.

Life I wish was different.
Different than it is.
It is not fair.
Not fair that I am here.
Here is where I don't want to be.
To be here is a travesty.
Travesty I wish I could avoid.
Avoid at all costs.
All costs lead to hell.
To hell I do not want to go.
Do not want to go but it is so tempting.
Tempt...
Te...

104. Northshore Park, Middle Bench, Facing the Water

Having the urge to jump in this water.
In this water,
I'm drowning.
Drowning out the noise.
The noise inside my head.
My head
filled with thoughts.
Thoughts I can't control.
Control,
I lost it all.
It all
doesn't make sense.
Sense I don't have.
Have the strength to go on.
Go on living.
Living in this hell.
This hell inside my head.
My head is under water.
Under water, I cannot breathe.
Cannot breathe but, it's okay.
It's okay because I'm drowning.
Drowning out the noise.

105. Crazy

First night I cried,
Next morning, I died
a little inside,
when they said I couldn't go home.
Took me upstairs,
in a wheelchair,
Like I wasn't capable of walking on my own.
The tears kept flowing
could barely tell them my name.
They told me the rules.
Took me to my room.
I laid there in silence.
Trying to keep sane.
Stared out the door,
watched them walk the floor,
around the nurse's station they go
so slow,
mumbling to themselves, yelling
about aliens, their family, each other.
Hear the attendings talk about what they're
going to get from the cafeteria,
wish I could go.
All I could do is stare out the door.

I kept to myself.
All I did was "rest"
and waited 'til I got to go home.
Ate, showered, slept, watched
repeat.
I just want my freedom given back to me.

106. Why Am I Here?

These people are crazy!
Why am I here?
"Time for dinner!"
I'm not hungry
but I rise from my laying position.
Walk down the hallway
making my way
to the end of the line.
Wonder what time
I'll be able to get out of here.
"BOYD!"
Grab my tray.
Find an empty seat.
Barely eat.
Return my tray.
Head back to my resting place.

He's not supposed to come in our room,
use our toilet,
pee all over the seat.
I don't feel safe.

I want to feel the sun's heat
upon my feet.
But I don't want to go outside unless I'm leaving.
When can I go?

Inside My Brain

Nobody seems to know.

"VITALS!"
Wakes me from my sleep.
Want to weep
I must stay strong.

Lay in bed.
Stare out the window.
Use the phone to call my people,
"Hey, Daddy! I love you!"
"Hey, Mommy! Don't worry!"
"Hey, Bae! I miss you!"
"Hey, sis! They're fighting, I have to go. Bye!"
Back to my room I trot
with only one thought,
When can I go?
Nobody seems to know.

Have a new roommate,
she's a little weird,
bathing every 5 minutes,
GOSH, I must get outta here!
When can I go?
Nobody seems to know.

Must bathe in the community shower,
keep my socks on
don't know what this floor has going on.
Water everywhere,
even on my clean clothes.
When can I go?
Nobody seems to know.

"BOYD! VISITORS!"

"Hey, Mommy! Hey, Bae!
I'm so happy y'all came today!"
"Hey, Mommy! Hey Daddy!"
"When can you go?"
"Nobody seems to know."
"TIMES UP!"
Back to my room I go.
Each time I watch them walk through those
double doors,
without me.

Four days of this.
Staring out the window.
"BOYD! FOOD!"
"VITALS!"
"VISITORS!"
Sleep.
Repeat.
When can I go?
Nobody seems to know.

Finally get to talk to the shrink.
"Why are you here?"
"Are you still having those thoughts?"
"Do you still want to kill yourself?"
"NO! I JUST WANT TO GO HOME!"
"Okay, you're free."
"Mommy and Daddy, come get me!"

Rush out those doors,
give my parents a hug and a kiss.
This place I surely won't miss.
Home, sweet home,
Nice hot shower,
food in my belly

that wasn't prepared in a cellar.
Cuddle on the couch.
Sleep in my own bed.
Still have nightmares of that place in my head.
Tear up thinking about what I went through.
Psych Ward, I will never forget you.

107. 600LB Life

Food is a drug,
and I'm addicted.

108. Little Sister

I never wanted to act like your mom.
Just wanted to keep you from doing wrong.
I came off a little strong,
you know me.
I wanted to keep you safe.
I should have been your go-to,
not judge you
Because who am I?
Not God.
You should have been able to talk to me
about ANYTHING
But I ruined that.
I want that back.
I wish you were still here.
We could lay in bed & talk about our fears,
watch movies, eat snacks, laugh about the
future and past in tears.
You said they help with your pain and
anxiety,
You should have talked to me.
I would have understood
You didn't think I could
so, you hid it from me.

Didn't trust me,
that hurts.
I forgive you
for it all!
Do you forgive me?
That's all I need.
I'll always be here for you
when you fall.
To help pick you back up on your feet.
Little sister,
please come back to me!

109. RIP Granny Sadie

It's been a year since Daddy called me,
said you had gone to glory.
Whole world came crashing down.
Had to run outside.
Tears fell from my eyes
like a broken hydrant.
Knees buckled.
Thankfully, the house was there to hold me
up.
Said he was on his way to get me
so, we could see
your body.
Then, I got a call from Granny Lee
"Did you hear the news about my mommy?
She has gone on to glory!"
Yes, I'd heard,
I'd gotten the word
that my best friend is no longer here with
me!
Daddy came and had to hold me up.
Jumped in the truck and rushed to you.
Walked in the room and ran back out.
Tears fell again like the remedy for a
drought.

I saw your body just lying there.
No life left.
My soul left.
I didn't wanna believe it was true.
Didn't wanna believe there was no more you.
I wasn't ready to give you up,
I needed more time!
But God needed you more.
Going to your house is still hard for me,
Filled with too many memories,
memories of you and me
laughing uncontrollably.
Wish you could come back to me
but I know you wouldn't even if you could.
My heart will never be the same.
I miss you.
I love you.
My best friend.
My laughing partner.
My pinching buddy.
My jokester.
My heart.
My soul.
My Granny.

110. Thank You

Thank you
for taking this journey with me.
Thank you
for letting me be free.
Thank you
for letting me express my inner thoughts.
Thank you
for letting me release my pain.
Thank you
for not judging me.
Thank you
for supporting me.
Thank you
for reading my poetry.
Thank you.

Inside My Brain